THEN & NOW®

NEW PORT RICHEY

OPPOSITE: Pictured in 1922 on Main Street, the two-story Ralph Werner Building was an active place of commerce in the downtown business district. Built in 1919, the second floor contained the first city hall after incorporation in 1924, rented for $10 a month. The Central Market, Beach's Music Store, and Bill Casey's Barber Shop were located on the first floor. (West Pasco Historical Society.)

THEN & NOW®

NEW PORT RICHEY

Jeff Cannon

This book is dedicated to everyone with the keen interest in preserving and learning from our historical past.

ISBN 978-0-7385-8816-2

Library of Congress Control Number: 2011928560

Published by Arcadia Publishing
Charleston, South Carolina

Printed in the United States of America

For all general information, please contact Arcadia Publishing:
Telephone 843-853-2070
Fax 843-853-0044
E-mail sales@arcadiapublishing.com
For customer service and orders:
Toll-Free 1-888-313-2665

Visit us on the Internet at www.arcadiapublishing.com

On the Front Cover: This photograph shows the city's popular Meighan Theater, named in tribute to silent movie star Thomas Meighan, who adopted New Port Richey as his favorite Florida city and owned a home on the river. Located at 6237 Grand Boulevard, the theater opened July 1, 1926, with the showing of Meighan's movie *The New Klondike*. Featuring live stage productions, it is now known as the Richey Suncoast Theater and still draws a crowd today. (Above, Jeff Cannon; below, Henry Fletcher.)

On the Back Cover: Taken on March 2, 1927, this photograph published in the *New Port Richey Press* shows a view of Main Street looking east from Dixie Highway (Grand Boulevard). The original caption from the paper reads as follows: "As this street view shows, New Port Richey's ratio of automobiles per capita is very high. The picture was made on Wednesday, when downtown traffic is not at all inflated." Today, *Press* reporters would be amazed at the automobiles per capita and the growth of downtown. (Henry Fletcher.)

Contents

Acknowledgments

It is impossible to name everyone who has contributed through the years, but for this book, I owe the greatest amount of gratitude to the West Pasco Historical Society Museum and Library for allowing me unlimited access to its physical and digital archives.

I'm very much thankful to the society's digital archivist, Jeff Miller, for his time and patience during my many visits to the museum to gather photographs from its collections or to return these from a previous trip, all during a time when the museum was closed for major renovations. I'm also grateful for his numerous email correspondences and for taking the time to proofread the book's final proofs.

I am also truly indebted to Henry Fletcher for graciously sharing his amazing New Port Richey postcard collection, as well as for the time he dedicated to meticulously scanning these images to the detailed specifications required for publication. Henry has always been enthusiastic about preserving the past images of our community, and without him, certain sections of this book would not be possible.

I also want to acknowledge my family and my parents, Danny and Barbara Cannon, for their years of support during my historic preservation work and research.

To everyone else in the community who offered support along the way, my thanks are endless.

Unless specifically credited otherwise, the earlier images are courtesy of the West Pasco Historical Society and all modern images were photographed by the author.

INTRODUCTION

In its infancy, New Port Richey was founded as a mecca where northern residents could come to escape the monotonous, dreary winters. Early on, every indication pointed to the rapid growth of the new Gulf Coast city, which was wholeheartedly supported by its residents, who cooperated in every movement for the advancement and betterment of New Port Richey. As a result, these hardy pioneers, mostly from the northern states, began to see their dreams come true. Among the greatest assets of the young city were the loyalty, optimism, and aggressiveness of its citizens and their confidence in the future of the city and surrounding country; this sentiment was also shared by the residents of Tampa, St. Petersburg, and other nearby cities. However, if not for the settlement of nearby Port Richey or advancement of timber operations by the local Fivay Sawmills, the city of New Port Richey might have never come to fruition, forever remaining a dream.

Between 1872 and 1874, the area's first settler, James Washington Clark, arrived on the coast from Brooksville, where he lived and operated a local meat market. Settling along the northern bank of the Pithlachascotee River, the Clark family constructed a home, and on December 2, 1878, James established the Hopeville Post Office, which was the first post office in the area. Soon after the Clark family arrived, Felix Sowers and his family settled west of the Clarks at the mouth of the Pithlachascotee River on a point of land overlooking the beautiful Gulf. Here, Felix built his family a simple home and planted orange groves. On January 20, 1883, both Clark and Sowers received titles to their properties after a cash purchase from the state; Clark paid 80¢ per acre for 80 acres, while Sowers paid $1 per acre for 76 acres. In December 1883, deciding to return to Atlanta where he originated, Felix Sowers sold his home and Gulf Coast interest to Aaron McLaughlin Richey, who arrived from St. Joseph, Missouri. Following his arrival, Richey acquired a schooner and established a small store, calling the location of his new home along the Gulf Coast "Richey Point." In May 1884, he applied for and received approval to establish Port Richey's post office, which replaced the previous Hopeville Post Office after it was discontinued on November 22, 1881. During this time, there wasn't a New Port Richey, as settlers referred to this prime hunting ground south of Port Richey as "Hickory Hammock."

On February 3, 1883, the state sold the lands known as Hickory Hammock, south of Port Richey, to the Florida Land & Improvement Company for 25¢ per acre as part of several hundred thousand acres that were purchased. Today, these lands contain part of the city of St. Petersburg and nearly all of the city of New Port Richey. By May 1883, the Florida Land & Improvement Company had conveyed a portion of this land, including land containing New Port Richey, to Anson P.K. Safford, company president and former territorial governor of Florida. In January 1885, Anson P.K. Safford deeded his lands to the Cooty Land & Improvement Company, a company that he owned and named after the Pithlachascotee River. After Safford's death in May 1897, the Cooty Land & Improvement Company sold its Hickory Hammock holdings to the B.F. Bullard and A. Sessoms turpentine operation for the extensive pine trees that grew there. Following Bullard and Sessoms's use of the land for turpentine, the property was then transferred to Aripeka Sawmill Company, a Georgia corporation that began the extensive cutting and milling of the pine trees from the land. With an extensive network of railroad trams, the pine timber was hauled to the company's Fivay Sawmills, a few miles northeast of present-day New Port Richey and where the town of Fivay sprang to life in the wake of the mills' operations. The Fivay Sawmills and town not only flourished but also paved the way for New Port Richey, which grew in place of the clear-cut pine trees that were removed from the acreage where the city now stands.

In preparations for the closing of their Fivay Sawmills in August 1911, the Aripeka Sawmill Company sold a large portion of its lands to Peter L. Weeks of Brooksville, who was actively involved in the area's turpentine industry along with his brothers. Peter, his brother Josiah S. Weeks Jr., and W.E. Guilford then formed the Port Richey Company with the purpose of colonizing and developing the lands along the Pithlachascotee River into a town site. Immediately following their acquisition, with the Weeks brothers acting as financial backers and W.E. Guilford as manager, the Port Richey Company began laying out plans for the new town site. On October 16, 1911, the company filed its plat map, titled *Plan for the Town of Port Richey, Florida*, with the Pasco County clerk. With the purchase of a 10-acre tract, the Port Richey Company offered one "house-lot" in town for free. While no significant development had yet occurred, the company advertised "a house in town gives the convenience of stores, railroad, post-office, churches, schools, the companionship of close neighbors, and society of friends. Exceptional natural conditions will cause the town to develop rapidly into an important city." The plans for the future city not only called out a specific lot for a hotel and railroad passenger station, but they also included numerous streets and avenues, although not named. According to *The Genesis of New Port Richey*:

> "The first few years after 1911 were trying and uncertain ones. Mr. Weeks was soon tired of pouring money into a proposition where everything went out, and nothing seemed to be coming in. Mr. Guilford, with cooling ardor and the impatience of all real dreamers, departed for other fields. From the fall of 1912 to the fall of 1913 Benjamin H. Hermanson, Mr. Robins, Gerben DeVries and M.L. Price were successively connected with the enterprise, each full of enthusiasm and doing his best, but, with no capital available, only sporadic attempts at colonizing could be made. Each brought in a few settlers, many of whom would have gone back if they had had enough money to get away.
>
> In January, 1915, Mr. Weeks, the owner of the property, in casting about for someone to relieve him of his load, met R.E. Filcher and George R. Sims, known as the firm of Filcher & Sims, and succeeded in interesting them in the property. But Filcher & Sims, busy with other developments in Florida, did not personally become identified with New Port Richey until the early part of 1916, when Mr. Sims, having acquired Mr. Filcher's interest, came here to live, and built his little bungalow overlooking the Cotee River and Enchantment [Sims] Park."

As early as July 1914, the use of the names "old Port Richey" and "new Port Richey" appear in news print. However, following a dispute in the delivery of mail from the Port Richey Post Office, on February 20, 1915, Gerben M. DeVries applied for and received approval to establish the New Port Richey Post Office, and the name New Port Richey became official. Over the next several years, the Port Richey Company replatted the former town of Port Richey into the town of New Port Richey, which was finally incorporated as a city in 1924.

CHAPTER 1

DOWNTOWN

Looking west from the water tower about 1923, the downtown business district at Main Street and Grand Boulevard (Dixie Highway) are visible. In the distance, smoke is rising from Gulf Utilities Company along the railroad tracks into town. Main Street didn't extend beyond the river, and a baseball field existed at the northeast corner of today's Bank and Main Streets. (Henry Fletcher.)

Among the first buildings constructed downtown were the Port Richey Company land office and railroad depot, shown below about 1914. Notice the boxcar parked at the depot in the background. The land office was originally erected in the middle of what would become Main Street but was later moved when roads were laid out and built. If the building still survived, it would be situated along Grand Boulevard just north of Main Street, shown above. (Below, DeVries Collection.)

With increased interest in the development of the downtown business district, the Port Richey Company sold its first land office building. Above is the land office building (center) after being sold and occupied by the Port Richey Lumber and Hardware Company. The Hotel Newport (Grand Rapids Inn) was constructed to the south of this building, and to the north the New Port Richey Drug Store, comprising the early downtown business district at the northeast corner of Main Street and Grand Boulevard (Dixie Highway).

During the early development of downtown, Main Street didn't extend beyond Dixie Highway (Grand Boulevard). Below is a view from the back of the New Port Richey Drug Store facing Grand Boulevard at the northeast corner of Main Street. Main Street ended here. To cross the river, a bridge was built at the southern edge of today's Sims Park. In 1927, the Main Street Bridge was constructed and the road extended west. The bridge is still in the same location today.

Below is another early view of Main Street from atop the Snell Building taken about 1920 that shows few buildings along the north side of the street. In the foreground is the second Port Richey Company land office, and in the middle is the H.H. Havens Building, constructed in 1915. Notice Orange Lake and Circle Boulevard in the background. The current view above shows the vast natural and man-made changes of the last 90 years with little evidence of the past.

On the south side of Main Street near Adams Street was the Snell Building, which featured a hall and meeting room upstairs. The Snell Building was the location of town hall meetings and meetings of Pearl of the West Lodge F&AM No. 146, First Baptist Church, and Community Congregational Church. In 1924, the residents of New Port Richey voted to incorporate the city while in this building.

Seen above in a photograph taken looking west down Main Street is the impressive two-story Snell Building. The structure stood prominently on Main Street, and if it survived today, it would be situated near the southwest corner of Adams Street. On the first floor was the City Market and New Port Richey's first library, established in 1919 as the Avery Library and Historical Society. Just west of the Snell Building and down Main Street was E.R. Washington's Feed Store, the small wooden building pictured at center.

Built in 1914, E.R. Washington's Feed Store was the city's first feed store, providing residents with hay, grain, feed, and bricks and cement, which were likely used during the community's earliest construction. In 1919, the feed store building was replaced with a two-story brick building owned by Ralph Werner and occupied by the Central Market. In 1939, the building shown below was constructed with aid from the WPA and housed the library, city hall, and fire department. (Above, DeVries Collection.)

Built in 1919 at the southeast corner of Main Street and Grand Boulevard, the building shown above was intended to be a new bank. In June 1919, the Port Richey Company moved into the building, making it the company's third land office, conveniently located next to the railroad depot. In the 1930s, this became the office of local real estate and insurance agent Michael Milbauer. Unchanged since constructed, the building stands today as an iconic reminder of the city's past.

Looking south along Grand Boulevard in the early 1920s, the photograph below shows how close the train depot was to the third Port Richey Company land office, now located at 5728 Main Street. The railroad tracks running along the bottom of the picture are today's Nebraska Avenue. Here, the land office was easily accessible to new land prospectors arriving to the city via the railroad or those arriving via the Dixie Highway (Grand Boulevard).

Replacing E.R. Washington's Feed Store on Main Street in 1919 was the brick two-story Ralph Werner mercantile building, shown above (center) just east of the land office (far right). Looking east down the Main Street block from Grand Boulevard, the recreation hall is the dark building, with Palms Theater in the distance next to the Snell Building. Below, a modern view shows the land office, the only surviving structure of that era, in the foreground. The other buildings were later replaced.

Situated at 6307 Grand Boulevard and now occupied by the downtown bar the Karl Reef is the two-story Clark Building. Built in 1922 by James Washington Clark Jr., the building originally accommodated four stores on the first floor with two 4-room apartments, one 5-room apartment, and one 6-room apartment on the second floor. After opening, J.H. Moran rented two stores on the first floor for his feed business.

Below, looking south on Dixie Highway (Grand Boulevard) towards the intersection of Main Street, the Clark Building stands prominently at the busiest intersection of the city. Photographed around 1923, not long after construction of the Clark Building, this was the perspective travelers of the Dixie Highway saw as they entered the city from the north. As the city's population grew, so did the downtown business district as seen above. (Below, Florida State Archives.)

In August 1921, after a failed attempt to organize a bank two years prior, the First State Bank of New Port Richey was organized and immediately began construction of a new building, pictured here at 5721 Main Street. Built by Largo contractor W.C. Newcomb, the building, made of fine stone, was constructed as nearly burglar proof as possible with necessary precautions taken during construction to make it as safe and secure as engineering could devise at the time.

At the northwest corner of Main Street and Grand Boulevard, the First State Bank was conveniently located in the growing downtown business district, as shown above. On June 13, 1931, the bank suspended operations as a result of the Great Depression, and it wouldn't be until 1952 that the city received another bank, Gulf State Bank, which opened in the same building. Today, the old building, no longer used as a bank, still survives as a business office.

Built in 1911–1912, the Sass Hotel, later known as Enchantment Inn, was among the most attractive buildings constructed downtown. The well-constructed frame building had wide verandas, a large office and dining room, and 10 to 12 bedrooms. Guests were within walking distance of downtown, the railroad depot, Enchantment (Sims) Park, and the river for easy access to boating and fishing. The hotel burned in 1926 in a spectacular midnight blaze. Today, the hotel would sit at 6345 Grand Boulevard.

Below is a view of Sass Hotel and downtown from the north side of Orange Lake. At the far right is the hotel. In the center, the train depot is barely visible behind the business block at the southeast corner of Main Street and Grand Boulevard. At far left is the back of the H.H. Havens Building and the second Port Richey Company land office, facing Main Street. Today, downtown is barely visible from the lake's north shore, although it is quite scenic.

Originally owned by Horace H. Havens, the two-story Havens Building, seen below, was constructed in 1915 at Main Street and Florida Avenue, serving as a grocery store, post office, and woodworking shop, with a hotel on the second floor. In 1925, the building was purchased by Mort Swafford, and thereafter, it became the Swafford Building. Some believe that the Havens-Swafford Building still stands today as the oldest commercial building in downtown, having been extensively altered to the structure pictured above.

While Swafford planned extensive alterations to the 1915 Havens Building on Main Street, it's believed that these plans never materialized. Instead, in its place, Swafford erected the architecturally attractive building shown above during construction in 1926. Also seen below, it appears today at 5749 Main Street. While the upper floor was a hotel, the first floor was home to many businesses, including a grocery, feed store, chamber of commerce, and billiards hall. Hotel names included the Rialto, Harmony Hotel, Just-A-Mere-Inn, and Chasco Inn.

On July 1, 1926, at a cost of $50,000, the city's Thomas Meighan Theater opened at the southwest corner of Grand Boulevard and Nebraska Avenue. The theater introduced live music in 1927 and talkies in the 1930s. Some time around 1934, the doors closed as a result of the Great Depression; however, they reopened in 1938. In 1972, the Suncoast Young People's Theatre purchased the building and opened it as the community-supported Richey Suncoast Theatre, which features live productions, carrying forward the theater's legacy.

In 1926, the two-story Leeston-Smith Building, above, was built along Grand Boulevard, adjoining to the south of the Meighan Theater. E.A. Leeston-Smith was also involved with the company that built the theater. At the time of the photograph below, occupants of the building included Bailey's 5, 10 & 25¢ Store and the Great Atlantic and Pacific Tea Company. Today, the Leeston-Smith Building serves a variety of uses, including office space, a restaurant, and an art gallery. (Henry Fletcher.)

Opposite the theater, the two-story Pasco Building was constructed in 1926 at the southeast corner of Grand Boulevard and Nebraska Avenue. Among the earliest tenants of the building were Roscoe's Drug Store, Pasco Hardware Company, a bakery, and rental apartments upstairs. In more recent years, the Pasco Building was home to the Café Grand restaurant, Boulevard Beef & Ale, several retail shops, a cocktail bar, and office space on the second floor.

Prior to the 1926 construction of the Pasco Building, the Buckeye Garage, above, was located at the southeast corner of Grand Boulevard and Nebraska Avenue. The dark-colored building at center is the train depot, which sat behind the third Port Richey Company land office at Main Street and Grand Boulevard. Acrcss from Buckeye Garage was the Dixie Filling Station, which sat where the theater is today. Barely recognizable, the photograph below shows the same basic perspective as it appears now.

As noted throughout, the railroad tracks into the city ran along today's Nebraska Avenue. Above, in a photograph taken looking west along the tracks, an early train is backed into the depot at the northeast corner of Grand Boulevard and Nebraska Avenue. With New Port Richey as the end of the line, trains had to back into the city from the only turnabout several miles south. Near Nebraska Avenue and Jefferson Street were the city's freight yard and end of the tracks. (Above, DeVries Collection)

Originally owned by the Tampa & Gulf Coast Railroad until sold to the Seaboard Airline Railway in 1927, tracks entered the city from the south, crossing the river in the area of today's Lafayette Street before proceeding in a northerly course into the area of Grand Boulevard and Nebraska Avenue and making a slight curve to the east and south into the area near the theater. Today, little evidence of the railroad exists except for the modern signs installed to create Railroad Square.

Located on what is now a parking lot on Nebraska Avenue behind the theater was the Gulf Utilities Company and Ice Plant, which operated from about 1919 to 1930 (electric service discontinued in 1923). Owned by Leland C. Poole, the power plant had three gas-powered engine generators. However, operation wasn't 24 hours a day; instead, the town's electricity was usually turned on about 5:00 a.m. and turned off at 11:00 p.m. This was also the location of the city fire department until 1939.

In 1939, the fire department moved into the building at 5740 Main Street with the library and city hall. With assistance from the Work Progress Administration (WPA), the new city hall, library, and firehouse building, above, was constructed on the same site as the previous E.R. Washington's Feed Store (built in 1914) and Werner Building (built in 1919). Part of the city's contributions to the project was salvaged materials from the torn-down Werner Building. Today, this building stands as a reminder of the past.

Above, the two-story New Port Richey Grammar School, built in 1915, sat at the northwest corner of Main Street and Madison Avenue. By 1919, the school carried the usual primary and normal grades and the ninth and 10th grades of junior high. By 1921, attendance had reached 102 students, taught by three teachers. In 1926, the dark green grammar school building was replaced with a modern redbrick school, occupied by the New Port Richey Public Library since 1991.

When constructed in 1926, the Pierce Grammar School, below, was modern in all respects. Serving the community for nearly 35 years, the school closed in the late 1950s, and students attended the Richey Elementary School on Madison Street, above, still used in 2011. In 1960, the city purchased the former Pierce School at 5939 Main Street for a city hall and municipal purposes. In 1991, the city's library moved into the building after construction of a new city hall/municipal building next to it.

In 1922, at a cost of $40,000, Gulf High School opened in New Port Richey, serving the county's west coast. When completed, it was a modern, two-story, redbrick school like Pierce Grammar. Gulf High remained at 5520 Grand Boulevard until 1961, when it was moved into a new building on Louisiana Avenue that is now Gulf Middle. Today, the 1922 Gulf High School building serves as the Schwettman Education Center, and it is still owned by Pasco County School Board.

On September 9, 1961, a new Gulf High School, relocated as a result of increased enrollment, was dedicated on Louisiana Avenue. After relocation, the old building on Grand Boulevard became the Gulf Junior High School; however, by 1970, both junior and high schools were in the same building on Louisiana Avenue, above. In 1971, a new junior high school was built on School Road, below, but in 1977, the junior and high schools switched campuses.

Worshippers endured chiggers and fleabites during the first religious services held in 1914 in Enchantment (Sims) Park. By 1915, construction of a church building, above, at the northwest corner of Pennsylvania Avenue and Jefferson Street, was underway, and it was completed by 1918. Started as a community church but completed with funds borrowed from the Methodist Episcopal Conference, it became the city's first Methodist church. Today, the church is located one block north of this original location.

In 1919, six years after starting the Our Lady Queen of Peace Catholic Mission with seven families, the first Catholic church in West Pasco was constructed on Washington Street by Fr. Felix Ullrich under the direction of the Benedictine Abbey of St. Leo. In 1966, the church relocated to its present facilities on US 19, and in 1992, a new police department was built on the Washington Street church lots after moving the historic church building to Sims Park.

From services at Enchantment (Sims) Park in 1914, five separate churches were established in the city; among them was the Community Congregational Church, with Rev. Milton Babcock as the organizing pastor in 1921. The first services were held in the Snell Building; however, in the summer of 1921, Meade Wood commenced construction on the building below facing Orange Lake on Circle Boulevard. Before completion, the building was badly damaged by a hurricane in the fall of 1921. Today, the church still resides at 6533 Circle Boulevard.

CHAPTER 2

ROADS, STREETS, AND BRIDGES

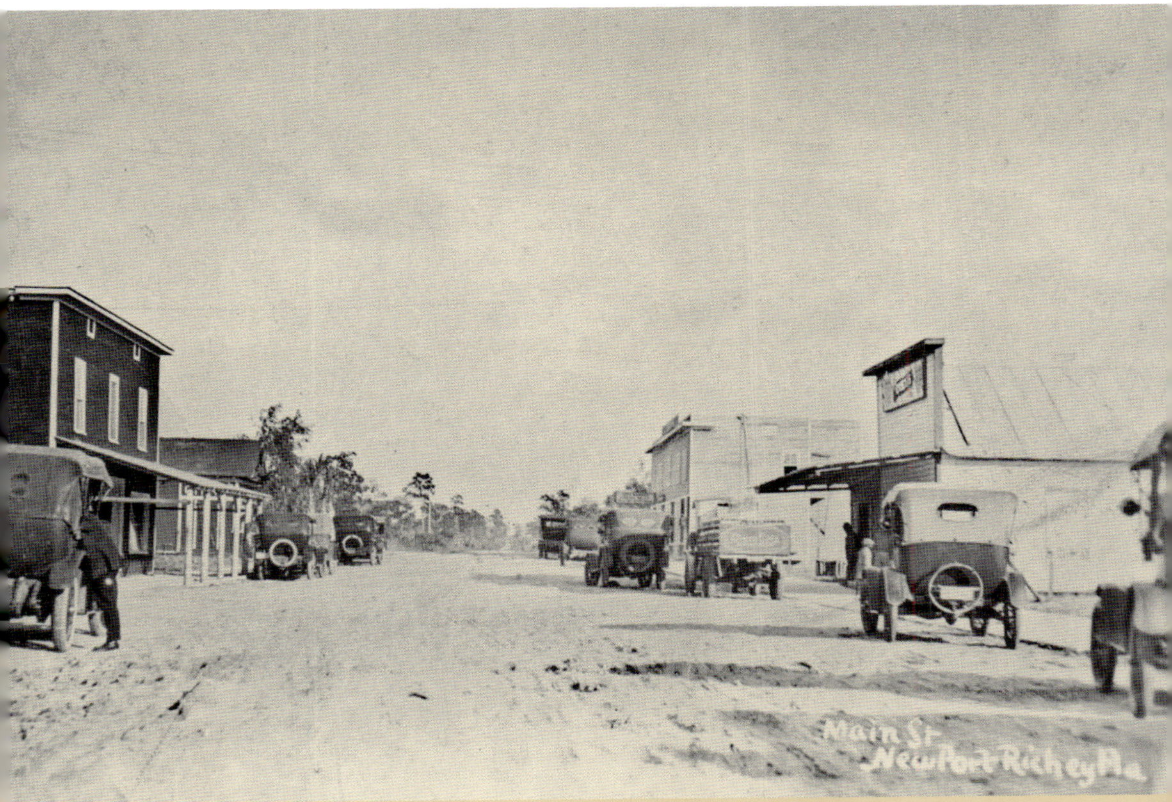

This photograph, taken about 1918 at the intersection of Florida Avenue, shows a busy Main Street downtown. On the left, or north, side of the street are the two-story H.H. Havens Building and Port Richey Company land office, later home to the *New Port Richey Press*. On the right, or south, side, E.R. Washington's Feed Store and Snell Building are in the distance.

The above photograph, taken in the late 1910s looking west towards downtown, shows the city's Main Street. The two-story building at right is the grammar school at the northwest corner of Main and Madison Streets. Travelers of these early roads would often get stuck in the deep sand ruts or on protruding palmetto roots. Today, some take the nicely paved roads for granted. Seen below is the same location today as cars speed by with no worries of becoming stuck.

While most roads in the city were dirt ruts leading to downtown, Main Street was better kept and included a curbed sidewalk. Below, facing west towards the intersection of Dixie Highway (Grand Boulevard), is an early view of Main Street through downtown. Notice that Main Street ended at Grand Boulevard and didn't extend west beyond the river. With the many original buildings gone, today's Main Street, above, is barely recognizable compared to the historic view.

Before Main Street's extension west beyond the river, residents crossed on the wooden Park Road bridge, below. The bridge was so named because of its location at the southern edge of Enchantment (Sims) Park along Park Road. Today, the road leading to the old bridge from town would pass through the middle of Sims Park, connecting to Bridge Road on the west side of the river. The Park Road bridge was replaced in 1927, when Main Street was extended.

As Main Street was extended west of the river, it became necessary to construct a new bridge. In February 1927, plans were approved for a modern concrete humpback bridge, above, situated about 260 feet south of the earlier Park Road bridge. Funded by the county, the new $30,000 Main Street Bridge was built by Quist Construction Company and opened September 1927, with Henry Quist and his family driving the first automobile across. The humpback bridge was replaced in 1967 with a more modern bridge. (Above, Henry Fletcher.)

The photograph above, taken facing west, shows today's Central Avenue (originally Michigan Avenue) as it appeared around 1920. Built in 1919, the two-story home on the left was owned by Gerben DeVries, the city's first postmaster, and it still stands today at 5914 Central Avenue, by the intersection with Jefferson Street. From left to right, the other two homes pictured were owned by the Brake and Stevens families. Below, now with a number of homes on the block, the current view is barely recognizable.

Below, looking southwest towards downtown, is an early view of Central Avenue just east of Adams Street. Located on lots 15 and 16, block 74, the two-story building at right was the second building constructed downtown, built by James Wallace McNatt and owned by William Raymond McNatt, his brother. Commonly called Idlewile by residents, the first floor contained a store while the second story had a meeting hall that was used for early school and church purposes.

Below is a c. 1920 view of the Cornell home at the southwest corner of Madison Street and Montana Avenue. Montana Avenue was first cleared by the Port Richey Company in 1919. Unlike most streets, Montana Avenue obviously had little traffic, apparent by the absence of two deep sandy ruts. Today, the Cornell home still survives at 5946 Montana Avenue; however, the street has taken on a new appearance over the last 90 years.

In January 1919, the Port Richey Company started working to clear and open several city streets, including Montana Avenue, Illinois Avenue, and Delaware Avenue from Madison Street to Dixie Highway (Grand Boulevard). These avenues all intersect with Jefferson Street, which was also cleared, completing a loop of cleared roads around downtown. Today, there has been very little deviation from the originally surveyed roads. In the image below, taken facing west, is the nicely paved Delaware Avenue at its intersection with Madison Street.

In 1916, the first rock road through downtown was completed; the Dixie Highway, now known as Grand Boulevard, cost $135,000. When complete, the western division of the Dixie Highway connected Montreal, Canada, with Florida; this section of highway through the city was a side scenic route of the main road. Today, the original Dixie Highway through Pasco County has been realigned to become the high-speed US Highway 19.

North of town, the Dixie Highway (Grand Boulevard) follows a route along the Pithlachascotee River. When the road was completed in 1916, the palmettos and scrub were so dense that one could not see 10 feet from the road and would never know the river was there until reaching a point just north of Virginia Avenue. Today, this is a most scenic route into the city. Seen below about 1920 is the Dixie Highway near the intersection of Orange Grove Avenue, and above is the same location today.

Below, looking north on its approach to the city from the south, is an early view of the original Dixie Highway (Grand Boulevard). Just beyond the curve, the road crosses the Pithlachascotee River at the present-day Boulevard Bridge. Today, this is the approximate location of where Gulf Drive intersects Grand Boulevard, shown above. All along the roadway, modern development has changed the landscape of the once-picturesque Dixie Highway. (Below, DeVries Collection.)

South of town, the Dixie Highway (Grand Boulevard) crossed the Pithlachascotee River via an iron and wooden bridge. Above, heading south in about 1919, is the perspective early travelers of the Dixie Highway would have seen as they approached the bridge. The road, only nine feet wide at the time, was wide enough for one car. Below, a current view of the bridge, now known as the Boulevard Bridge, shows the road has grown to a width of more than 50 feet. (Above, DeVries Collection.)

In 1916, when construction of the Dixie Highway (Grand Boulevard) through town was completed, the iron-and-wood bridge at the southern edge of town was modern in all respects. Above, pictured from the river looking west, the simple truss construction of the iron bridge is seen. This bridge spanned the Pithlachascotee River for more than 30 years until being replaced with a more modern concrete bridge in 1956.

Below is another early view of the Dixie Highway (Grand Boulevard) bridge as it spans a peaceful Pithlachascotee River south of town. Looking east, it is evident that the old iron-and-wood bridge was actually constructed as two spans sitting on large concrete pillars in the river. In 1957, the iron-and-wood bridge was replaced with the concrete bridge shown above, which is still in use today. (DeVries Collection.)

On March 18, 1939, the iron and wooden Boulevard Bridge south of town was crushed and partially collapsed under the weight of a 17-ton gasoline truck that was attempting to cross. The truck, not extracted for two days, drew a continuous crowd of curious onlookers. The bridge was eventually repaired, and damaged planks were replaced. In the above photograph, taken from the same location, modern bridges have mandatory weight restrictions to prevent such a collapse.

The Boulevard Bridge was closed for a week after the 1939 collapse. After the 17-ton gasoline truck was extracted, the state road department worked day and night for four days to repair the bridge, as seen above. Repairs to the bridge were performed by guarded prison crews, typical of how all Florida roads were maintained. The modern concrete bridge at the same location is shown below. Obscured by trees, the old Gulf High School is no longer visible from the bridge.

While originally called Dixie Highway, through-town maps named the road the Boulevard, now known as Grand Boulevard. Early residents often referred to the downtown section of the Boulevard as "Depot Street" because of the location of the railroad depot at the northeast corner of the Boulevard and Nebraska Avenue. In the 1970s and 1980s, the section of road through town lying south of Main Street was referred to as South Boulevard, while the section to the north was known as North Boulevard.

CHAPTER 3

ORANGE LAKE

One of the city's early natural attractions was Orange Lake, situated at a central point in the original town site of about one square mile. Actually a sinkhole, not a lake, the community's early settlers called this Blue Sink because of its pristine blue water. This little lake was also known as a prime hunting ground where residents frequently shot bear, deer, wild cats, and alligators.

Taken about 1915, the photograph below shows an early view of Orange Lake and the first few homes that were built on the northwest shore. At this time, Circle Boulevard was nothing more than a sand trail leading to the homes. Notice the horse grazing at the lakeside. From left to right are the homes of Vaino Malstrom, Will Bragg, and James Casey. Today, this is the intersection of Washington Street and Circle Boulevard, as seen above.

In the above view, taken looking northwest about 1920, Circle Boulevard had been improved, while a number of new homes overlooking the lake had been built. The name "Mirror Lake" was mistakenly written on this postcard by the photographer; Mirror Lake is in the center of St. Petersburg. Today, most homes along Circle Boulevard are obscured by trees planted for privacy or trees that have been allowed to grow around the lake.

The c. 1916 photograph above, taken looking west towards today's Sims Park, shows an interesting perspective of Orange Lake. This photograph, taken soon after the completion of the Dixie Highway in 1916, shows the work made to clear the lakeshore so that passersby could enjoy its natural beauty as they entered the city from the north. Today, many still enjoy the natural beauty of Orange Lake and the circle walk that has been built around it. (Above, Henry Fletcher.)

Driving south along Dixie Highway, among the first thing travelers would see on their approach to town was Orange Lake and the grand Sass Hotel built on the lake's southern shores. Below, an early view of the Sass Hotel shows Orange Lake in the foreground and Dixie Highway fenced in on the far right. Today, if the hotel still survived, it would be nestled between Bank Street and the boulevard. However, in 1926, it burned to the ground in a spectacular midnight blaze.

Looking north from atop of the Hotel Newport in the c. 1918 photograph below, the beautiful Orange Lake is centered in the downtown area. With most of the trees removed from the lakeshore, one could see for about a half-mile. The lake had been fenced to prevent livestock from being eaten by alligators. Above is a similar view looking northeast with the addition of a fountain and numerous trees. (Above, Jeff Miller; below, Henry Fletcher.)

In 1929, the city's municipal golf course opened, consisting of 18 miniature greens surrounding Orange Lake and managed by professional golfer Gene Sarazen. Above, with downtown barely visible in the background, a group of golfers enjoys a round on the greens. The course was open to the public seven days a week, free of charge. In 1935, voters decided 131 to 29 to close the municipal golf course, and today, there is little evidence of its existence except for a few planted palms. (Above, Henry Fletcher.)

After the May 1926 burning of the Enchantment Inn (Sass Hotel), outlines for a new community hotel were made. Plans called for a modern 50-room hotel of extreme Spanish design, equipped with a steam heating plant and comfortably furnished throughout. The new hotel would be called the Hacienda. On August 12, 1926, ground was broken for the new hotel, and when completed, it sat poignantly overlooking Orange Lake and the Cotee River at the edge of Enchantment (Sims) Park. (Above, Henry Fletcher.)

CHAPTER 4

HACIENDA HOTEL

With a construction cost of $100,000 and an additional $30,000 in furnishings, the Hacienda Hotel formally opened on February 17, 1927, only 184 days after the ground-breaking. This photograph shows an early interior view of the Hacienda foyer, its fine furnishings, and the dining room in the background. In October 1996, the Hacienda was added to the National Register of Historic Places. (Author's collection.)

On February 5, 1927, the Hacienda was thrown open for an informal inspection by residents and guests alike prior to the formal opening of the hotel. With a crowd of 800, the first guests were welcomed and dinner was served—turkey, cornbread, corn, and all the trimmings. Above is the back entrance to the now-vacant old hotel, and below is the front of the Hacienda as it appeared shortly after opening. (Below, Henry Fletcher.)

Another view of what used to be the front of the hotel shows it nestled under the moss-draped oaks and leaning palms. The Hacienda was the scene of many brilliant social affairs and assembled some of the most famous writers and living celebrities of stage and screen, including Thomas Meighan, Leon Errol, Madeline Cameron, Frances Ring, Flora Zabelle, Bob Davis, George Ade, Ring Lardner, and Hal W. Lanigan. Today's visitors to Sims Park seldom realize the hotel's early significance to the city. (Above, Henry Fletcher.)

Guests to the Hacienda not only had convenience to the river, Orange Lake, and nearby Jasmine Point Golf Course, but they also had opportunity to spend some time on the greens of the hotel's miniature golf course, as shown above. The road pictured in the foreground is today's Bank Street, originally called Riverside Place. The former hotel's miniature golf course is now a parking lot and an entrance to Sims Park, as pictured below. (Above, Henry Fletcher.)

Built with community money, the Hacienda Hotel survived the Great Depression; however, in the years that followed, the hotel's ownership changed as stocks were bought and sold. It originally fronted Sims Park, but in the 1940s, the entrance to the hotel was shifted to Main Street. Pictured below from a 1957 city directory is a view of the Hacienda's Main Street entrance. The same view today shows that the hotel yard has been paved over for a parking area.

Below is another interior view of the Hacienda, showing the spacious dining room where guests gathered for home-cooked meals served by the hotel's proprietor. Not only was the dining room used by hotel guests, but it was also the scene of various community events, such as the city's 50th anniversary celebration in 1974. After the hotel closed, the interior was extensively remodeled. The image above, captured in 2007, is the renovated dining room entry looking into what used to be the hotel foyer. (Above, Jeff Miller.)

After nearly 60 years of service as a hotel, the Hacienda closed in 1985, following an announcement that Gulf Coast Jewish Family Services, Inc., had selected the site for Florida's first House for Special Services—a 75-bed facility housing elderly persons with mental disabilities. Pictured above in 2000 is the former hotel during its use by Gulf Coast Jewish Family Services, Inc. In August 2003, the building was purchased by the city for $2.2 million, and it has subsequently been vacant. (Above, Jeff Miller.)

With all of its splendor and history, the Hacienda Hotel was added to the National Register of Historic Places on October 24, 1996, while still in use as an assisted living facility. However, since being purchased by the city in August 2003 for $2.2 million, the former hotel has been vacant, and as a result, vandals and time are taking their toll on the historic property. Today, residents are concerned about the future of the historic Hacienda Hotel as it remains vacant.

CHAPTER 5

Enchantment Park/ Sims Park

In 1911, when the town site was surveyed, plans were made for Enchantment Park, which was to be located between Orange Lake and the Cotee River. In January 1915, this park became a reality when the land was cleared of underbrush and planted with grass seeds. Today, residents know this park as Sims Park.

The c. 1920 image below shows the natural beauty of early Enchantment Park. Taken from the park entrance and looking east towards Orange Lake, this photograph shows the Hermanson home, located near the corner of Circle Boulevard and Central Avenue, in the background at right. Today, this is the location of the museum and library of the West Pasco Historical Society and the historic Our Lady Queen of Peace Hall.

Believed to have been taken in 1922 from the Park Road bridge during one of many water carnivals celebrated by residents, the photograph above offers an interesting perspective of early Enchantment Park on the right. A glimpse of the earliest seawall is also provided as residents park their cars along the riverbank in preparation for the carnival events. Seen in the distance is the community boat launch. Today, residents still enjoy the park and a scenic walk along the river.

In December 1924, park ownership transferred from the Port Richey Company to the city with other conveyances of lands comprising the city. By resolution, the town council voted unanimously to change the park's name to Sims Park. The park included a tennis court, small croquet field, a community boat launch, and a boathouse, as well as a gazebo originally owned by George Sims. The community clubhouse was nearby. Extensively remodeled, the boathouse gazebo was moved and now resides in front of the museum and library of the West Pasco Historical Society, below.

CHAPTER 6

Pithlachascotee River

Pictured here in December 1919, several residents enjoy a winter dip in the river. For centuries, the enchanting beauty of the river has attracted many. Commonly called the Cotee River, the source of this river's name is said to be of Seminole-Creek origin; with *pithlo* meaning "canoe" and *chàskita* meaning "to chop" or "to cut," it is fully interpreted as "the river where canoes are made."

Pictured below and taken from the Park Road bridge is a photograph of the picturesque Cotee River. Barely visible on the right is the community clubhouse, and in the distance is the community boathouse and gazebo, both situated in Sims Park. The west river bank, as left, appears as it was before being developed as part of Jasmine Point. Throughout the history of the city, there has been an attempt to keep the river's natural beauty for visitors and residents to enjoy.

At its source, the Pithlachascotee River begins several miles northeast of the city at Crews Lake. After flowing through several thousand acres of wooded and pristine pasturelands, the river meanders through the city on its way to the Gulf. Today signs of development are all along the banks of the Cotee River. The photograph above, taken facing west from the Boulevard Bridge, shows the once jungle-like appearance along the river; the image below of the same view today shows the extensive development.

On its approach to the Gulf, not only did the river widen, but it also passed through some of the most beautiful flat woods in Pasco County, containing an opulent amount of wildlife. Nearing the Gulf, the banks of the river changed as saw grass grew amidst the dense palmettos and scrub oaks. The river possessed an unharnessed amount of beauty and what seemed to be an infinite supply of fish. Today, that beauty has been captured by the city on the river.

Pasco County's first coastal highway, the Dixie Highway, offered early automobile travelers a most scenic route. On its approach to the city, Dixie Highway followed a course that was laid along the eastern bank of the Cotee River. Below is an early view looking northwest toward the Cotee River as it parallels the Dixie Highway at Moonlight Bay. Today, at the same location, the scene very much resembles those of days past.

The area of the Cotee River referred to as Moonlight Bay is located along today's Grand Boulevard (Dixie Highway) at a deep bend in the river near the northern city limits between Port Richey and New Port Richey. Below is another early view of the Dixie Highway at Moonlight Bay. Pictured above is a view of the same location showing the riverbank lined with homes. Visible in the distance is the US Highway 19 bridge, built to replace the outdated wooden bridge of past.

Just west of Moonlight Bay, the Cotee River meanders past Port Richey before entering the Gulf of Mexico. Seen above about 1920 is the Clarks-Nicks home, built in 1912 on the banks of the river in Port Richey. Today, part of this home still exists, although a current photograph of the same location is barely recognizable due to the vast man-made changes and development along the riverbanks. The large building to the far right is Catches Waterfront Grille. (Above, author's collection.)

Prior to the deepening of a channel at the mouth of the river by the Army Corps of Engineers in 1925, the river was completely blocked by a huge oyster reef, signs of which are still evident today. Looking from the river southeast towards today's Sunset Drive, the photograph above offers an interesting perspective of the river. One of the homes on the right, which still survives today, was once owned by June Carter and Johnny Cash, inherited from June's mother, Maybelle.

Near the mouth of the river, Sunset Drive parallels the river's southern bank just west of present-day US 19. The c. 1920 photograph below, taken looking west, shows Sunset Drive as it appeared long before its modern improvements of asphalt and seawalls. Today, this road still follows its original scenic route along the river, and one thing that remains unchanged is the number of private docks accessing the river, as shown above.

Looking west towards the Gulf from the Oelsner Indian Mound at the mouth of the river, one can see the natural beauty that attracted many early settlers to the area. The dock pictured below, owned by the Oelsners, was destroyed during the No-Name Storm of 1993 and replaced with the dock seen above. Notice the areas that were once mangroves and marsh are now covered with condominiums and homes overlooking the river and Gulf waters.

Today at the mouth of the river is a small island called Durney Key, made from dredging spoils of the 1970s. Durney Key, shown below in the background, was named for John H. Durney, who served as mayor of Port Richey (1967–1975) and mayor of New Port Richey (1978–1980) and was instrumental in the dredging of a channel for boat traffic. Dredging spoils also extended the mainland, where huge homes are now built. Above is a view at the mouth of the river about 1920.

In the Gulf, just beyond the mouth of the Cotee River, are numerous historic stilt-house fish camps. A complete fishing camp surrounded by the Gulf waters, many of these stilt houses were first constructed in the 1930s and 1940s. Grandfathered in, owners of these camps have entered into a lease with the state for use of the sovereign and submerged lands beneath them, while new camps cannot be established. (Above, West Pasco Historical Society, Jane Baillie Collection.)

Since the earliest development along the river banks, residents have constructed docks from which to enjoy the beauty of nature, park their boats, or to simply fish. As development along the river increased, so did the number of docks, as evident above. To protect properties from erosion, owners also installed seawalls, which today span nearly the entire length of the river through the city. Below, about 1920, a man enjoys fishing from one of many primitive docks along the river, believed to be near Moonlight Bay.